CLEARWATER / ST. PETERSBURG
The Delaplaine
Long Weekend Guide

TABLES OF CONTENTS

Chapter 1
WHY CLEARWATER /
ST. PETERSBURG?

It's really all about the beach here in Clearwater, which consistently ranks among the top beaches in the U.S. (Look over any survey of "best beaches" and the ones here typically show up year-after-year.)

CLEARWATER / ST. PETERSBURG

The Delaplaine
2021 Long Weekend Guide

Andrew Delaplaine

NO BUSINESS HAS PAID A SINGLE PENNY OR GIVEN *ANYTHING* TO BE INCLUDED IN THIS BOOK.

A list of the author's other travel guides, as well as his political thrillers and titles for children, can be found at the end of this book.

Senior Writer - **James Cubby**

Gramercy Park Press
New York London Paris

Please submit corrections, additions or comments to
andrewdelaplaine@mac.com

Embedded on the Pinellas Peninsula are excellent beaches strung out along 25+ miles of barrier islands.

Clearwater is at the northern end. At the south end is St. Petersburg Beach, the more crowded and congested of the cities here.

Moving north to Treasure Island, things get quieter as you go over to Sand Key. Here you have Indian Shores, Madeira Beach, Redington Shores, Bellair Beach. Crossing the high bridge here takes you to Clearwater Beach.

St Petersburg derives its name from the city of the same name in Russia because one of its founders, Peter Demens, was from there. Demens was a pivotal figure in the development of St. Petersburg because he helped get rail service established in the late 1880s, spurring growth.

There are wildly juxtaposed entities here: you'll find kitschy souvenir shops in the same area as the world headquarters of Scientology. Spring training brings the Philadelphia Phillies, who offer their games at Bright House Field, not far from the site of the original Hooters restaurant. Go figure.

The lifestyle in Pinellas County is decidedly more laid back than Miami and the East Coast cities in South Florida. That's why people like it.

You will too.

Chapter 2
WHERE TO STAY

I have several friends of mine who do this in Miami, on South Beach where I live, and they are all happy with the entire experience.

ALDEN SUITES
5900 Gulf Blvd, St Pete Beach, 727 360-7081
www.aldenbeachresort.com
Located on 5 acres overlooking the Gulf, this resort offers 140 suites with all the comforts of home (except you get a maid every day). Amenities include: free daily newspapers, free parking, tennis, state-of-

the-art 12-person hot tub, high-speed wireless internet access, and flat-screen TVs. Activities include: basketball, shuffleboard, volleyball and ping pong. Two heated pools.

BAYVIEW PLAZA WATERFRONT RESORT
4321 Gulf Blvd, St Pete Beach, 727-367-2791
www.plazabeachresorts.com
Located directly across the street from the beach, this family owned and operated resort features just 7 suites. A charming and affordable small boutique resort. Heated pool overlooking the bay. Fitness room and fishing pier. Most rooms have private balconies.

THE BEACHCOMBER BEACH RESORT AND HOTEL
6200 Gulf Blvd, St Pete Beach, 727-367-1902
www.beachcomberflorida.com
They have a private sandy beach with over 5 acres of lush tropical gardens. Sports bar, beach bar and live music. This resort offers a variety of activities, comfortable accommodations, two outdoor swimming pools, Jimmy B's Beach Bar, live entertainment and dancing. Amenities include: High speed wireless internet access, 25-inch TVs, Fitness Center, Data Port Phones, and Business Center. Non-smoking rooms available.

THE BIRCHWOOD
340 Beach Drive NE St, St Petersburg, 727-896-1080
www.thebirchwood.com
NEIGHBORHOOD: Downtown

This classically decorated boutique hotel offers 18 modern guestrooms. Amenities include: complimentary Wi-Fi, flat-screen TVs, iPod docks, complimentary continental breakfast and bottled water. Hotel facilities include: on-site restaurant, bar, and rooftop lounge. Non-smoking & pet-free.

DOLPHIN BEACH RESORT
4900 Gulf Blvd, St Pete Beach, 727-360-7011
www.dolphinbeach.com
Located right on the Gulf, has a pool with sundeck, 173 rooms, Flippers Beach Bar, Boca Sands Grill, and 400 feet of sandy beach. Activities include: shuffle board, parasail, and variety of water sports. Free pool lounges. All rooms include microwave, refrigerator, satellite TVs, in-room coffee maker and hair dryer.

FRENCHY'S OASIS MOTEL
423 E Shore Dr., Clearwater, 727-446-6835
www.frenchysoasismotel.com
This small 15-unit is a "retro boutique" property, located 3 blocks from the world-famous beach. This renovated property features a variety of spectacular amenities, including rooms with fully equipped kitchens, a 40″ flat screen TVs with Blu-Ray player, MP3 player docking stations, Terrazzo flooring and stunning views of the Florida Intracoastal Waterway from private balconies. Guests are greeted with a welcome package including complimentary menu items from all four French's Restaurants and **Clear Sky Café**.

GRAND PLAZA HOTEL RESORT
5250 Gulf Blvd, St Pete Beach, 727-360-1811
www.grandplazaflorida.com
This luxury hotel and beach resort is one of St
Petersburg's best. Features three beachfront
restaurants: Spinners, The Palm Room and Bongos
Beachside Bistro as well as a poolside and beachfront
bar. The Grand Plaza is the tallest hotel along the
Gulf of Mexico in St Pete. Amenities include: Free
parking, Fitness Center, free wireless high-speed
internet access, free local newspaper, free coffee and
tea in the lobby, 32 inch TVs, and DVD/CD players.
All renovated beach resort guestrooms feature a
private balcony with incredible views of the coastline.
Conveniently located near fishing, golf, museums,
and parks.

HOTEL ZAMORA
3701 Gulf Blvd, St Pete Beach, 727-456-8900

www.thehotelzamora.com
NEIGHBORHOOD: St Pete Beach
This white-washed Mediterranean palace offers
luxury accommodations – many with balconies
overlooking the Gulf of Mexico. Amenities include:
walk-in spa showers, complimentary Wi-Fi, outdoor
pool, cable TV, and complimentary bottled water and
daily newspapers.

THE HYATT REGENCY CLEARWATER BEACH RESORT AND SPA

301 S Gulfview Blvd., Clearwater Beach, 727-373-1234
www.hyatt.com
Why do some hotels have such damn L-O-N-G
names? Whatever you call it, this Hyatt is a beautiful
waterfront hotel and resort that offers luxurious
lodgings in a sleek contemporary West Indies style.
Poolside cabanas come equipped with Wi-Fi Internet
access, a high definition flat screen TV and a
secluded veranda. Every guestroom is a suite is a
condo-style apartment with full kitchen and walk-out
balconies offering water views.

THE PONCE DE LEON HOTEL

95 Central Ave, St Petersburg, 727-550-9300
www.poncedeleonhotel.com
This Mediterranean boutique hotel offers a charming
tropical get-away featuring 79 guest rooms on five
floors. This is an Earth friendly, green and non-
smoking property. Amenities include: flat screen
cable TV, wireless internet, microwaves, mini-bars,
and in-room coffee makers. Conveniently located

near nightlife, attractions, restaurants and art galleries.

THE POSTCARD INN
6300 Gulf Blvd, St Pete Beach, 800-237-8918
www.postcardinn.com
NEIGHBORHOOD: St Pete Beach
Hip hotel with 196 guestrooms. The owners converted an old-style Colonial Gateway Inn into this very retro spot featuring surfboards in the rooms, a photo booth in the lobby, nice touches like that. Reasonable. Amenities: Complimentary Wi-Fi, flat-screen TVs, and complimentary toiletries. On-sight **Boathouse Kitchen and Bar**, **PCI Beach Bar** and **Snack Shack**. Private beach, outdoor pool and fitness center.

RUMFISH BEACH RESORT
6000 Gulf Blvd, St Pete Beach, 800-360-4016
www.tradewindsresort.com
NEIGHBORHOOD: St Pete Beach
Located on the sands of St Pete Beach, this resort offers beautiful accommodations – each guest room and suite a different look. Amenities include: flat screen HDTVs, wet bar, and wireless internet access. The resort features include: on-site restaurant with a 33,500 gallon aquarium, indoor/outdoor bars, live entertainment, retail shop, whirlpool, and two swimming pools. Lots of activities for kids.

SANDPEARL RESORT

500 Mandalay Ave., Clearwater Beach, 727-441-2425
www.sandpearl.com

Most of the bigger and better lodgings in these parts
are owned by big corporations. This one is locally
owned. When you arrive here, they give you a glass
of sparkling wine while a player piano bangs out
tunes in the background. This beachfront resort offers
year round relaxation and comfort. Activities are
boundless from the climate controlled zero-entry pool
to the beachfront fire pits. Rooms feature high
definition flat screen televisions, alarm clocks with
iPod / MP3 dock, wireless and wired Internet access.
Onsite restaurant and full service spa.

SHERATON SAND KEY RESORT

1160 Gulf Blvd., Clearwater Beach, 727-595-1611
www.marriott.com

Has 24-hour guest services. They handle everything
from golf tee times to dinner reservations, Scuba

diving, parasailing, jet skiing, sailing, deep-sea fishing charters, local sightseeing, and tickets for theater and sporting events; transportation needs. Has 10 acres of private beach. Rent a cabana, beach chair, or WaveRunner. Heated beachside pool and

whirlpool, beach volleyball, and a children's playground. Fully equipped tennis complex, which includes three lighted all-weather courts in a unique gulf-front location. The Suncoast Fitness Center, located on our top floor, offers a fully equipped state-of-the-art fitness center in a modern environment with spectacular views of the beach and bay. Work out on the newest CYBEX equipment or simply enjoy the benefits of a sauna or a massage.

VINOY RENAISSANCE ST. PETERSBURG RESORT & GOLF CLUB

501 5th Avenue NE, St. Petersburg, 727-894-1000
www.marriott.com
NEIGHBORHOOD: Downtown

Gorgeous and luxurious 4-star Mediterranean Revival resort with 361 spacious rooms that has perhaps the most unrivaled view of the downtown waterfront. The story goes that in 1923 famed golfer Walter Hagen accepted a bet from oil millionaire A.V. Laughner that he couldn't hit a golf ball off Laughner's pocket watch without breaking the crystal. He hit several balls off the watch with no damage. Someone suggested Laughner ought to build a nice hotel where the balls had landed, in an empty lot across the street. He spared no expense, and gave the hotel his middle name, Vinoy. President Coolidge and Babe Ruth stayed here, as well as Marilyn Monroe. The place fell into disrepair and was closed for a couple of decades until a big renovation brought the place back to its former glory. **Marchand's Bar & Grill** features hand-stenciled floor-to-ceiling windows. The rnd Ballroom now has a fabulous Chihuly chandelier. The 3-story high vaulted ceiling in the lobby was similarly restored. It's fun to take the tour several times a week at 10:30. Amenities include: Flat-screen TVs, Complimentary Wi-Fi and plush bedding. Four on-site restaurants besides Marchand's, a private golf course, spa, health club and outdoor pool. Conveniently located near Museum of Fine Arts and The Pier.

WATERGARDEN INN AT THE BAY
126 4th Ave NE, St Petersburg, 727-822-1700
www.innatthebay.com
NEIGHBORHOOD: Downtown
Set on an acre of lush landscaping, this inn in an old Victorian mansion dating to 1910 offers 14 beautifully decorated rooms and suites. Amenities include: complimentary Wi-Fi and coffee. Conveniently located near local shopping, restaurants, museums, and sports venues. On-site swimming pool.

Chapter 3
WHERE TO EAT

400 BEACH SEAFOOD & TAP HOUSE
400 Beach Drive, St Petersburg, 727-896-2400
www.400beachseafood.com
CUISINE: Seafood, Steakhouse, American
DRINKS: Full Bar

SERVING: Lunch & Dinner
PRICE RANGE: $$
NEIGHBORHOOD: Downtown St Petersburg
Led by Chef Tyson Grant and Chef Sean Squires, this 9,000 square foot eatery offers a nice varied menu and extensive wine list. Try the shrimp fritters, something you don't see on many menus. Also the smoke fish spread here is really tasty. Oysters Rockefeller and Mahi Mahi. Restaurant includes a tap room with 24 draft beers.

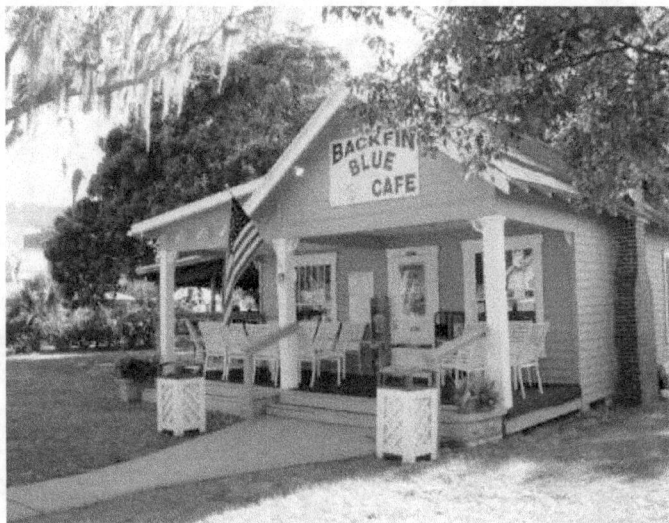

BACKFIN BLUE CAFÉ
2913 Beach Blvd S, Gulfport, 727-343-2583
www.backfinbluecafe.com
CUISINE: Seafood
DRINKS: Beer & Wine Only
SERVING: Dinner
PRICE RANGE: $$

NEIGHBORHOOD: Gulfport
Nice casual dining spot. Menu favorites include the
Backfin Blue Club and Tomato and Artichoke heart
salad. This place is known for their Crab cakes and
Crab Corn Chowder - both quite tasty.

BELLA BRAVA
204 Beach Dr NE, St Petersburg, 727-895-5515
www.bellabrava.com
CUISINE: Italian
DRINKS: Full Bar
SERVING: Lunch, Dinner
PRICE RANGE: $$
NEIGHBORHOOD: Downtown St Pete
Casual no-frills restaurant with typical Italian dishes
like pizza, flatbreads, pastas, chicken and seafood.

BOB HEILMAN'S BEACHCOMBER

447 Mandalay Ave., Clearwater, 727-442-4144
www.heilmansbeachcomber.com
CUISINE: Seafood, American (Traditional)
DRINKS: Full Bar
SERVING: Lunch & Dinner
PRICE RANGE: $$$

A Clearwater institution since 1948 and open every day of the year. Tasty menu items like hot brown and down-on-the-farm chicken. Great martinis. Stone crab claws are a specialty here. People often comment on the "Mad Men" ambience of this place because when you walk in here, it's like you're going back in time. Lots of people drink stiff martinis and lounge around the requisite piano bar and they even drop off relish trays at your table. (Remember them?) The steaks are sizzling, even if the atmosphere is retro.

BODEGA

1120 Central Ave, St Petersburg, 727-623-0942
http://eatatbodega.com/
CUISINE: Cuban/Latin American
DRINKS: Full Bar
SERVING: Lunch & Dinner; dinner only on Sat
PRICE RANGE: $
NEIGHBORHOOD: Downtown

A casual eatery with a chalkboard menu offering award-winning cuisine. Known for its excellent Cuban sandwich. (The bread they use comes from Ybor City's **Casino Bakery**.) Vegetarian and vegan options available. You can have a lot of fun at the rum bar. The fresh juices are made tangy by adding items like ginger or chili.

CAFE PONTE

13505 Icot Blvd #214, Clearwater, 727-538-5768
www.cafeponte.com
CUISINE: American (New)
DRINKS: Full Bar
SERVING: Lunch & Dinner
PRICE RANGE: $$$
NEIGHBORHOOD: Clearwater
Upscale elegant spot with white tablecloths that uses
a wall of their wine selections as a part of the décor to
good effect. Has an outdoor area under what looked
to me like a huge oak tree providing a canopy – a
good place to choose when the weather's good, and it
usually is here in Clearwater. Basically, they offer a
'New American' menu with a tasting-menu (that
looks like an early bird special designed as a tasting
menu) and a la carte option with certain items thrown
in to give it a vaguely "international" feel – ahi tuna,
charcuterie board with figs, things like that. Favorites:
Short Ribs and Lobster en Croute. Creative desserts.
Vegetarian Friendly, Vegan and Gluten Free Options.

CARRABBA'S ITALIAN GRILL

2680 Gulf-to-Bay Blvd., Clearwater, 727-712-0844
www.carrabbas.com/
CUISINE: Italian
DRINKS: full bar
SERVING: lunch / dinner
PRICE RANGE: $$
They turn out consistently reliable Italian specialties
here. Even though it's a big chain, it doesn't feel like
it.

CASTILE
Hotel Zamora
3701 Gulf Blvd, St Pete Beach, 727-456-8660
www.castilerestaurant.com
CUISINE: American / Southern / Spanish
DRINKS: Full Bar
SERVING: Breakfast / Lunch / Dinner / Brunch on weekends
PRICE RANGE: $$$
NEIGHBORHOOD: St Pete Beach
Located in The Hotel Zamora, this popular eatery offers an upscale beach dining experience. Nice menu with favorites like Roasted Chicken and Black Grouper Cheeks. Creative cocktails. Rooftop lounge.

CIRO'S SPEAKEASY & SUPPER CLUB
2109 Bayshore Blvd, Tampa, 813-251-0022
www.cirostampa.com
CUISINE: American
DRINKS: Full Bar
SERVING: Dinner
PRICE RANGE: $$$
NEIGHBORHOOD: SoHo
The prohibition-theme adds a bit of fun to this New American restaurant. Make a reservation so you get the secret password. Creative American fare with favorites such as Chicken and Waffles and Duckfat fries. Great cocktails.

CLEARWATER OYSTER COMPANY
655 S Gulfview Blvd, Clearwater, 727-451-1134
www.clearwateroystercompany.com

CUISINE: Seafood
DRINKS: Full Bar
SERVING: Breakfast, Lunch, & Dinner
PRICE RANGE: $$
NEIGHBORHOOD: Clearwater Beach
Unpretentious simply decorated seafood eatery
serving locally sourced products. Always a good
selection of oysters on its raw bar. Favorites: Pot Pie
with Maine Lobster & Scallops; Chopped Pork BBQ
Plate; Smoked fish Dip; Popular breakfast spot with
offerings like Shrimp & Grits; 'Hangtown Fry' (eggs,
fried oysters, crispy pork belly, toast); Southern fried
chicken & waffles.

COLUMBIA
1241 Gulf Blvd., Clearwater: 727-596-8400
800 2nd Ave. N.E., St. Petersburg: 727-822-8000
www.columbiarestaurant.com
CUISINE: Cuban / Spanish
DRINKS: full bar
SERVING: lunch / dinner

PRICE RANGE: $$

Place has been open since 1905 and claims to be "Florida's oldest restaurant." Well, whatever they've been doing, they haven't slacked off in all these years. Makes a Cuban sandwich from a 1915 recipe. Spanish Bean Soup is to die for. Scallops "Casimiro" features large scallops baked in a clay casserole dish with lemon butter topped with seasoned breadcrumbs. (All their shrimp come from Gerard Thomassie's family-owned Poor Pierre Shrimp of Louisiana.)

CRISTINO'S COAL OVEN PIZZA
1101 S Fort Harrison Ave., Clearwater, 727-443-4900
www.cristinospizzeria.com
CUISINE: Pizza
DRINKS: Beer & Wine
SERVING: Lunch & Dinner
PRICE RANGE: $$

Small but comfortable dining. Great pizza and pasta dishes. You have to try their delicious gelato.

FRENCHY'S

41 Baymont St., Clearwater Beach, 727-446-3607

www.frenchysonline.com

CUISINE: Seafood

DRINKS: Full Bar

SERVING: Lunch & Dinner

PRICE RANGE: $$

While they have 4 of these in the area, this is the original location and you'll like this small, quaint place featuring many of Frenchy's original menu items, like the smoked fish spread, seafood gumbo, boiled shrimp and Greek salad. Been here since 1981.

FRESCO'S WATERFRONT BISTRO
300 2nd Ave NE, St Petersburg, 727-894-4429
www.frescoswaterfront.com
CUISINE: Seafood
DRINKS: Full Bar
SERVING: Breakfast, Lunch, Dinner
PRICE RANGE: $$
NEIGHBORHOOD: Downtown St Pete
Located at the foot of the Pier, this is a casual seafood restaurant with a great outdoor area – seating and bar. Menu favorites include: Blackened Grouper Sandwich, Ahi Tuna and Portobello Tower – a layered vegetables dish. Great tropical cocktails and revolving menu of specials.

HAVEN
2208 West Morrison Ave, Tampa, 813-258-2233
www.haventampa.com
CUISINE: American
DRINKS: Full Bar
SERVING: Dinner only; closed Sun
PRICE RANGE: $$$

NEIGHBORHOOD: SoHo
Great comfortable eatery offers a great dining experience. Menu favorites include: King Crab Leg Dumplings and Braised Octopus. Bar features over 300 bourbons, 40 wines by the glasses and an impressive selection of cheeses and charcuteries.

ISLAND GRILL AND RAW BAR
210 Madonna Blvd, Tierra Verde, 727-767-0020
www.islandrawbar.com
NEIGHBORHOOD:
CUISINE: Seafood/Raw Bar
DRINKS: Full Bar
SERVING: Lunch, Dinner, Breakfast on Sat & Sun
PRICE RANGE: $$
NEIGHBORHOOD: Tierra Verde
If you happen to have been out fishing and caught something, bring your catch here and the chef will cook it for you. But they have their own great selection of seafood dishes. Fresh oysters (raw or cooked). The place is quite large, with plenty of sating indoors and out on the patio overlooking the water. Indoor and outdoor bars as well. Favorites: Lobster Mac & Cheese, Lobster bisque, Moscow Oysters, Key Lime Pie with a very sweet Graham cracker crust.

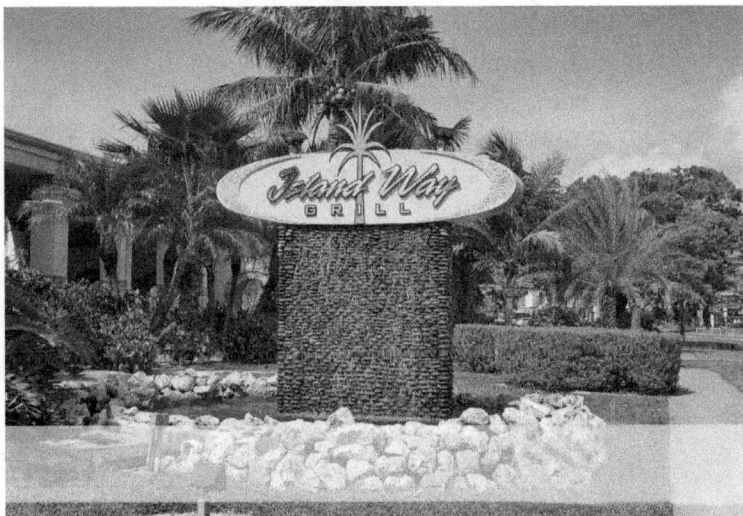

THE ISLAND WAY GRILL

20 Island Way, Clearwater: 727-461-6617
www.islandwaygrill.com
CUISINE: American / Brunch; Sushi Bars, Seafood,
Steakhouses
DRINKS: full bar
SERVING: dinner nightly; brunch on Sunday
PRICE RANGE: $$-$$$

Try the ultra-casual Brunch here. (You can even show
up barefoot.) Oysters from the Gulf, sushi made while
you wait, bottomless cappuccinos, smoked amberjack
fish spread, peel-and-eat shrimp. Owner Frank Chivas
buys his fish from local fishermen, so you know
you're getting the best available. During the winter
stone crab season, this is a must stop. (Near the
Aquarium. Overlooks Clearwater Harbor.)

JIMMY'S FISH HOUSE & IGUANA BAR

521 S Gulfview Blvd, Clearwater, 727-446-9720
www.jimmysfishhouse.net
CUISINE: Seafood/American Traditional
DRINKS: Beer & Wine
SERVING: Breakfast, Lunch, & Dinner
PRICE RANGE: $$
NEIGHBORHOOD: Clearwater Beach
Casual eatery with a popular bar on a huge outdoor
deck overlooking the water as well as the nearby
beach. Great place to watch the boats go by or to have
happy hour while watching the sun go down. Usually
has some live music out here as well. The seafood-
focused menu has lots of American comfort food
options. An awful lot of bad fried food options (fried
calamari, fried fish, fried shrimp, fried everything);
also plenty of junk food like fried mozzarella sticks,
nachos with your choice of glop on top; even the fish
in the fish tacos is fried. The usual big burgers. There
are some good options, however, with good oysters
on their raw bar, boiled & chilled shrimp; a few
salads to choose from.

LEVEL 11 ROOFTOP ARTISAN BISTRO BAR

5250 Gulf Boulevard, St. Pete Beach, 727-360-1811
www.grandplazaflorida.com/dining/level11
CUISINE: Tapas/Pizza
DRINKS: Full Bar
SERVING: Lunch, Dinner
PRICE RANGE: $$
NEIGHBORHOOD: St Pete Beach
No question that you'll want to watch sunsets from
this cute little rooftop bistro/bar specializing in tacos

and pizza. You'll get stunning views of the Gulf, of Boca Ciega Bay and, once it's dark enough, the sparkling lights of St. Petersburg. It's a nice crowd you'll be in, too, with young and old, all intently watching the sun slip into the sea. Sometimes people applaud when it finally sinks. Lots of fun. Assorted seafood dishes like: Ahi Tuna Tartare and Key Lime Shrimp Ceviche. Cocktails and wine list. Local beers.

MAD FISH
5200 Gulf Blvd, St Pete Beach, 727-360-9200
www.madfishonline.com
CUISINE: American, Seafood
DRINKS: Beer & Wine Only
SERVING: Dinner
PRICE RANGE: $$
NEIGHBORHOOD: St Pete Beach
This casual, upscale retrofit diner offers an innovative menu of classic American cuisine and comfort food. Menu favorites include: Char-Grilled Ahi Tuna Steak and Premium Oysters and Oysters Rockefeller. The key lime pie is the best.

MARCHAND'S BAR & GRILL
Renaissance Vinoy Resort & Golf Club
501 5th Ave NE, St Petersburg, 727-824-8072
www.marchandsbarandgrill.com
CUISINE: American (New)
DRINKS: Full Bar
SERVING: Dinner
PRICE RANGE: $$$
NEIGHBORHOOD: Downtown St Pete

This award-winning restaurant serves American cuisine with a "Floribbean" flair. The menu includes fresh seafood, braised meats and delicious sides. Great specials. Live music. Sunday brunch. For brunch try the innovative EGGS IN A JAR -Anson Mills Lil Moo Cheese Grits, Poached Eggs Corn Meal Fried Rock Shrimp and Roasted Chili Hollandaise all served in a jar. Every bite of this dish was perfect. Since it was served in a jar, you were able to get the right amount of egg, yolk, shrimp, grits and cheese. For dessert you must order the Smore's Cheesecake.

MARITANA GRILLE AT THE DON CESAR
Loews Don CeSar Hotel
3400 Gulf Blvd, St Pete Beach, 727-360-1882
www.maritanagrille.com
CUISINE: New American
DRINKS: Full Bar
SERVING: Dinner
PRICE RANGE: $$$$
NEIGHBORHOOD: St Pete Beach
This is the signature restaurant of the Loews Don CeSar Hotel and features large saltwater aquariums filled with colorful Florida fish. The cuisine is American with an emphasis on seafood. Menu favorites include: Orange Habanero Barbecued Grouper and Seared Diver scallop with a short rib agnolotti. Nice wine list.

MEL'S HOT DOGS
4136 E Busch Blvd, Tampa, 813-985-8000
www.melshotdogs.com
CUISINE: Hot Dogs
DRINKS: No Booze
SERVING: Lunch, Dinner
PRICE RANGE: $
NEIGHBORHOOD: Busch Gardens
If you like hot dogs you'll love this place. Try Mel's
Special Hot Dog (beef hot dog with sauerkraut,
onions, pickle, mustard and relish). The French fries
are crisp and well worth the calorie.

MFA CAFÉ
Museum of Fine Arts
255 Beach Dr NE, St Petersburg, 727-822-1032
www.mfastpete.org
CUISINE: New American
DRINKS: Beer & Wine Only
SERVING: Brunch, Lunch

PRICE RANGE: $$
NEIGHBORHOOD: Downtown St Pete
Located inside the Glass Conservatory of the
Museum of Fine Arts. Great spot for a gourmet lunch
or weekend brunch. Menu includes variety of
artisanal-crafted salads, sandwiches, soups and daily
specials. Everything here is hand made including the
potato chips and salad dressings.

MOON UNDER WATER
332 Beach Dr NE, St Petersburg, 727-896-6160
www.themoonunderwater.com
CUISINE: Pub, British
DRINKS: Full Bar
SERVING: Lunch, Dinner
PRICE RANGE: $$
NEIGHBORHOOD: Downtown St Pete
Café with a British pub type of vibe with indoor and
outdoor seating. Here you'll find typical British fare
(and some surprisingly good Indian cuisine as well).
Menu favorites include: Shepard's Pie, Sweet walnut
salad with chicken; also chicken curry.

NOBLE CRUST
8300 4th St N, St. Petersburg, 727-329-6041
www.noble-crust.com
CUISINE: Italian/Southern/Pizza
DRINKS: Full Bar
SERVING: Dinner, Weekend Brunch, Closed on
Mondays
PRICE RANGE: $$
NEIGHBORHOOD: St. Petersburg

Modern eatery, with an unpretentious interior and a lively bar scene in what can be a cacophonous room, offering a menu that mixes Italian and Southern fare. (You don't often see Southern Fried Chicken on the same menu as you do Gnocchi, and maybe for good reason.) Favorites: Rigatoni & Short Rib Ragu; Bianca Pizza (though there are several nice ones to choose from); 4-cheese grits (get this as a side order). Indoor and outdoor seating, communal tables. Vegan, vegetarian and gluten-free options. Happy hour.

O'MADDY'S BAR & GRILLE
5405 Shore Blvd, Gulfport, 727-323-8643
www.omaddys.com
CUISINE: American, Seafood
DRINKS: Full Bar
SERVING: Lunch, Dinner, Late Night
PRICE RANGE: $$
NEIGHBORHOOD: Gulfport
Located across from the beach, this casual grill offers a nice menu with great appetizers and daily specials.

Menu favorites include: Jessie's crab cake sandwich and Ahi Tuna. If you have the guts, indulge in one of their fun desserts – Donut O-rings and Deep Fried Twinkies.

OZONA PIG
311 Orange St, Palm Harbor, 727-773-0744
www.theozonapig.com
CUISINE: Barbeque
DRINKS: Full Bar
SERVING: Lunch, Dinner
PRICE RANGE: $$
NEIGHBORHOOD: Palm Harbor
Located in the heart of historic Ozona, this restaurant serves "Southern Style BBQ." BBQ fans will love the hickory smoked slow cooked BBQ Ribs. All the food is homemade and delicious with 4 choices of BBQ sauce. Great breakfast with homemade muffins.

PARKSHORE GRILL
300 Beach Dr NE #104, St. Petersburg, 727-896-9463
www.parkshoregrill.com

CUISINE: American/Seafood
DRINKS: Full Bar
SERVING: Lunch, Dinner, & Brunch
PRICE RANGE: $$
NEIGHBORHOOD: Downtown
Upscale eatery offering an impressive menu (one of
the better menus in town, according to me) of steaks
and seafood. The bar area has a few high-top tables so
you can eat in there if you like. (I like.) They have a
lot of outdoor seating (I don't like) but you're
basically overlooking a parking lot, as this is in a
modern big mall type setting, so there's not much to
look at. Favorites: Meatballs Stuffed with Blue
Cheese; Lobster Toast; Steak (several cuts); Bacon-
wrapped Meatloaf; Grilled Veal Chop; Roasted
Chicken Panini; Crab Cakes Dinner. Vegetarian and
gluten-free options.

PICO ROJO ROTISSERIE
2475 N McMullen Booth Rd., Clearwater, 727-474-
3826
http://picorojo.com/
CUISINE: Ethnic Food, Latin American
DRINKS: Beer & Wine
SERVING: Lunch & Dinner
PRICE RANGE: $
This family owned restaurant features Latin American
Rotisserie Chicken and foods cooked in an ecological,
natural and flavorful way. Delicious flavorful chicken
is a must-try.

RED MESA CANTINA
128 3rd St S, St Petersburg, 855-265-0812

www.redmesacantina.com
CUISINE: Mexican
DRINKS: Full Bar
SERVING: Dinner
PRICE RANGE: $$
NEIGHBORHOOD: Downtown
This modern Mexican eatery offers great food and large portions. Restaurant includes outdoor patio where you can chow down on traditional dishes like churrasco, ceviche and carne asada. Great selection of hand-crafted cocktails.

ROCOCO STEAK
655 2nd Ave S, St. Petersburg, 727-822-0999
www.rococosteak.com
CUISINE: Steakhouse
DRINKS: Full Bar
SERVING: Dinner nightly (bar opens at 4), Brunch on Sundays
PRICE RANGE: $$$$
NEIGHBORHOOD: Downtown
Located in a 1920s mansion that from the outside looks like a tarted-up funeral home. Inside, however, lights are low enough at night to offer a somewhat romantic atmosphere. This upscale steakhouse offers an impressive menu of grass-fed beef, as well as nicely prepared seafood, and small plates. Favorites: Scallops with asparagus; Raw Bar selections; Chilean sea bass; Steaks in a large variety—rib eyes, filet, strips, even a big Porterhouse. All the usual side dishes you expect in a fancy steakhouse these days. Crafted cocktails and extensive wine list given a Wine Spectator Award.

SALTY'S ISLAND BAR & GRILLE

437 S Gulfview Blvd, Clearwater Beach, 727-216-8085

www.saltysisland.com

CUISINE: Seafood

DRINKS: Full Bar

SERVING: Breakfast, Lunch, & Dinner

PRICE RANGE: $$

NEIGHBORHOOD: Clearwater Beach

Ultra-casual eatery with two levels—from the upstairs level you can sit outside and see the beach across the street. Nothing fancy. Has one of those HUGE menus it takes a few minutes to absorb, seeming to offer everything (anything?) you might want, from breakfast (eggs Benedict in 3 styles; b'fast tacos, Build Your Own Omelet) to lunch and dinner menus that have everything from the junk food nachos you expect in places like this to a wide variety of choices from BBQ ribs and chicken to pasta dishes to seafood platters, fish & chips, etc. I do really like the Hog Snapper Imperial (pan-fried snapper topped off with lump crab meat in a white cream sauce). Other Favorites: Grilled Gulf Grouper and Oyster Sampler. Happy Hour with live music.

SEA PORCH
Loews Don CeSar Hotel
3400 Gulf Blvd, St Pete Beach, 727-360-1881
www.doncesar.com
CUISINE: American / Southern / Cuban
DRINKS: Full Bar
SERVING: Breakfast / Lunch / Dinner
PRICE RANGE: $$
NEIGHBORHOOD: St Pete Beach
A popular eatery with typical American fare, less fussy than the other restaurant in the Don CeSar, the well-regarded **Maritana Grill**. The Sea Porch is just a few feet off the beach, making it a good choice for breakfast or brunch. Has some Cuban-inspired dishes. Southern favorites include: Cheese Grits Casserole and Low Country Shrimp and Grits. They serve a variety of breads including gluten-free.

SPEGGTACULAR
770 S Gulfview Blvd, Clearwater Beach, 727-401-3507
www.speggtacular.com
 CUISINE: American (New)/Breakfast
DRINKS: Full Bar
SERVING: Breakfast & Lunch

PRICE RANGE: $$
NEIGHBORHOOD: Clearwater Beach
The name says it all. This is a breakfast spot but also
serves lunch in a strip mall atmosphere where they
even have outdoor counter service created by pushing
up a couple of hurricane shutters. Traditional
breakfast with a variation on almost everything.
Favorites: Breakfast Club sandwich and Raison bread
French toast served with mixed fruit and English
cream. Great cocktails.

URBAN BREW AND BBQ
2601 Central Ave, St Petersburg, 727-623-9823
www.urbanbrewandbbq.com
CUISINE: Barbeque/American (Traditional)
DRINKS: Beer & Wine
SERVING: Lunch, Dinner
PRICE RANGE: $$
NEIGHBORHOOD: Grand Central District
Only place in town serving craft beer with craft BBQ.
Weekly specials. Favorites: Brisket Pork sandwich,
Skillet mac & cheese and Pork Belly sample. You can
get craft beer from the local favorite, **Rapp Brewing
Company**.

WILDFLOWER CAFE
1465 S Fort Harrison Ave., Clearwater, 727-447-4497
www.wildflowercafe.net
CUISINE: Breakfast, Brunch
DRINKS: Beer & Wine
SERVING: Breakfast & Brunch
PRICE RANGE: $
Delightful brunch spot with an outdoor patio. Great food and service. Delicious items like honey chicken salad, French toast and a variety of vegetarian items.

Chapter 4
WHERE TO SHOP

ARTPOOL GALLERY & VINTAGE BOUTIQUE
2030 Central Ave, St Petersburg, 727-324-3878
www.artpoolgallery.com
NEIGHBORHOOD: Grand Central District, Midtown
St. Petersburg's only art gallery with a vintage
clothing boutique, coffee shop, beer bar and vinyl
record shop.

BEING – THE ART OF LIVING
RELOCATING-CHECK WEBSITE, St Petersburg,
727-510-7375
www.shopbeing.com

Located on the edge of St Petersburg's historic old Northeast neighborhood, this gift shop features home interior accessories, rugs, lighting, and textiles. You'll also find gift items like artisan jewelry, hand-poured candles, fragrances, art & design books. Professional design services available.

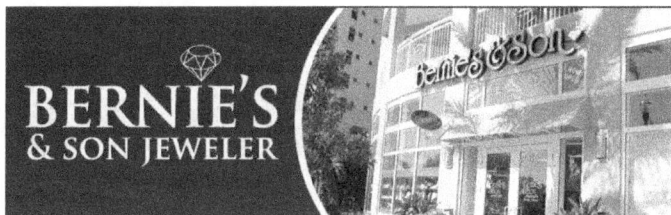

BERNIES & SON JEWELERS

154 Beach Dr NE, St Petersburg, 727-823-2000
www.berniesandsonjeweler.com
Family owned and operated jewelry shop selling estate and one-of-a-kind custom jewelry. Here you'll find wedding and engagement rings, gemstones, handcrafted Italian cameos and classic timepieces. This shop carries designer lines including: Bellarri, Teuffel, Natalie K, Cherie Dori and Van Lachman. Jewelry repair service.

FLORIDA CRAFT ART
(formerly FLORIDA CRAFTSMAN)
501 Central Ave, St Petersburg, 727-821-7391
http://www.floridacraftart.org/
A unique 2,000 square foot gallery/retail space that
specializes in specially crafted pieces and designs in
clay, wood, fiber, glass and jewelry. Revolving
exhibitions of regional, national and emerging artists.
The second-floor features 18 artists' studios and
classroom where workshops are offered. Closed
Sunday.

HASLAM'S BOOKSTORE
2025 Central Ave, St Petersburg, 727-822-8616
www.haslams.com
Florida's largest bookstore boasts over 300,000 books
including a large selection in almost every category.
Here you'll find new books, old books, and
collectible sets.

OXFORD EXCHANGE
420 W Kennedy Blvd, Tampa, 813-253-0222
www.oxfordexchange.com
NEIGHBORHOOD: Hyde Park
A unique combination of restaurant, shop with lots of decorative items and even a bookstore located in what used to be a 19th Century stable. Great place to meet, drink, and share your knowledge of literature.

THE SATURDAY MORNING MARKET
101 First St SE, St Petersburg, 727-455-4921
http://www.saturdaymorningmarket.com/
This fresh market offers fresh fruits and vegetables, arts and crafts, and variety of food. Live entertainment. Here you'll find farmers selling their wares as well as interesting crafts. Open on Saturdays, 9 am – 2 pm from early October to late May in Al Lang Field Parking Lot. In Summer (June to August), the market moves to Williams Park and is open 9 am-1 pm.

SHAPIRO'S GALLERY OF CONTEMPORARY AMERICAN CRAFTS
300 Beach Drive NE, St Petersburg, 727-894-2111
www.shapirogallery.com
Located across the street from the St Petersburg Museum of Fine Arts, this 3,000 square foot gallery/retail space offers the work of over 250 artists and craftsman including jewelry, wooden boxes, clocks, pottery, clay, glass, wood, metal, Judaica, mobiles, kaleidoscopes and outdoor art for the patio and garden.

SQUARESVILLE
3224 W Bay to Bay Blvd, Tampa, 813-259-9944
www.squaresvilletampa.com
NEIGHBORHOOD: South Tampa
Open years, this shop has offered over 1500 square feet of vintage fashions and unique mid-century home furnishings. Here you'll find poodle skirts, tie-dye shirts, go-go dresses, and men's platform shoes. The shop also features wigs, hats, sunglasses, and great costumes.

SURF STYLE
315 S. Gulfview Blvd., Clearwater Beach, 888-787-3789
www.surfstyle.com/
Note: has **multiple locations** in Clearwater area. Women's clothing, lots of swimwear. Nike, Speedo, Sketchers and BodyGlove, skateboards, surfboards, wakeboards, skimboards.

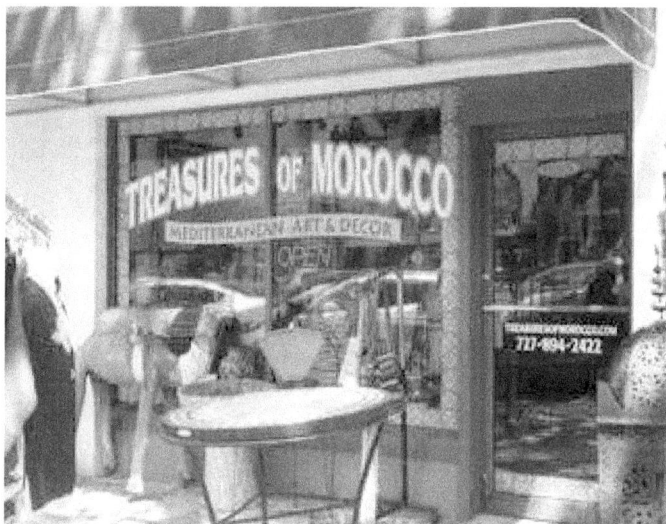

TREASURES OF MOROCCO
4039 7th Terrace S, St Petersburg, 727-894-2422
www.treasuresofmorocco.com
Beautiful boutique featuring work of artisans of
Morocco including rugs, lamps, mirrors, tiles,
ceramics, fountains, mosaic tables, furniture, colorful
kaftans, pottery, kitchenware and home accessories.
Here you'll find beautiful pieces from the talented
craftsmen of Morocco.

TWIGS & LEAVES
2253 1st Ave S, St. Petersburg, 727-822-5400
www.twigsnleaves.com
NEIGHBORHOOD: Grand Central District, Midtown
Specializes in native Florida plants, trees and flowers
and in fact was one of the first nurseries in Florida to
feature all-native plants. Also available:

environmentally friendly organic soils, fertilizers and
pesticides. Workshops and landscape seminar as well.

Chapter 5
WHAT TO SEE & DO

As far as Attractions go, I certainly don't expect you to remain in Clearwater for your whole trip, so I've included some things to do in the Tampa bay Area.

ADVENTURE ISLAND
10001 N. McKinley Dr., Tampa, 813-884-4386
www.adventureisland.com
ADMISSION: Adult - $85, Child -$77

HOURS: Check website for hours: Normally Mon. –
Thurs. 10 – 5, Weekends later.
A fun-filled water park filled with adventures like
corkscrew slides, waterfalls, a giant wave pool, a
rambling river, and other family attractions. 30 acres,
2 pools, 10 water slides, and 3 children's areas.

BUSCH GARDENS TAMPA BAY
10165 N McKinley Dr., Tampa, 813-884-4386
www.buschgardens.com
ADMISSION: Adults, Children 10 & Up - $75 Single
Day, Children 3-9 - $67
HOURS: 10 a.m. – 6 p.m.
Busch Gardens Tampa Bay combines world-class
thrill rides, Broadway-style live entertainment and
one of North America's largest zoos in an
unforgettable adventure for the whole family. New

this year, Iceploration features world-class skaters, larger-than-life puppets and even animal stars, inspiring audiences to "explore the world " on a journey to the four corners of the earth. Also new, the Animal Care Center welcomes guests to closely observe veterinary care and treatment at this new state-of-the-art facility, a 335-acre 19th century African-themed animal park. It opened on March 31, 1959 as an admission-free hospitality facility for Tampa Anheuser-Busch; in addition to various beer tastings they had, a bird garden and the Stairway to the Stars which was an escalator that took guests to the roof of the brewery.

Busch Gardens continued to grow and in 1965 they opened the 29 acre Serengeti Plains which allowed the African wildlife to roam freely. It continued to focus on its tropical landscape, exotic animals, and amusements to draw visitors. Busch Gardens began charging admission as the entertainment became more complex, with extra fees for the thrill rides, such as the roller coasters for which Busch Gardens is now known. Currently Busch Gardens competes with other such parks in Florida and charges comparable fees. The park is operated by SeaWorld Parks & Entertainment, owned by the private equity firm The Blackstone Group. In 2011, the park hosted 4.3 million people, placing in the Top 20 of the most-visited theme parks in the US and in the Top 25 worldwide.

The Serengeti Express (a replica steam train) runs along the back end of the park and makes stops at the Nairobi, Congo and Stanleyville themed areas. The train track was recently renovated, and its tracks have been changed.

The Skyride transports guests between Crown Colony and Stanleyville.

Morocco

The park's main entrance is home to the Mystic Sheiks of Morocco brass and percussion ensemble. Treats can be purchased at the Sultan's Sweets and the Zagora Cafe. The Moroccan Palace, a 1,200 seat indoor theatre, is located here, as well as the outdoor Marrakesh Theater. Gwazi is the major ride in this area.

Gwazi, a 105-foot, 50 mph dueling wooden roller coaster named after a mythological creature with the head of a tiger and the body of a lion opened. The dueling sides consist of a lion side and a tiger side, which cross paths seven times. In 2011 Busch Gardens replaced the original trains, which were boxy and sat four per coach. The new trains seat two per coach and should provide a smoother ride. Great Coasters International Inc. designed both the original Gwazi trains and the new Gwazi trains.

Gwazi Gliders, a small hang glider flat ride relocated from the Congo section's defunct Pygmy Village kids area.

Bird Gardens
This is the original section of the park that opened

back in 1959. The area for the most part remains to be mostly gardens and animal exhibits/shows. A staple attraction that once stood in this section was the brewery. However, the brewery closed in 1995 and Gwazi now sits where the brewery was located. The traditional, educational bird show is currently being replaced with a newer, more entertainment-based show, including a number of mammals.

Walkabout Way

Themed as an Australian outpost, Walkabout Way opened in June of 2010. This area gives guests the chance to see and hand-feed kangaroos and wallabies. This area is home to a kookaburra, magpie geese and Australian black swans. This experience is open to all guests 5 years of age or older.

Sesame Street Safari of Fun

Former Land of the Dragons children's section of the park. Land of the Dragons was replaced by Sesame Street Safari of Fun on March 27, 2010. It contains all the attractions from Land of the Dragons which are now re-themed. It also contains four new attractions: Telly's Jungle Jam, an interactive play area; Rosita's Djembe Fly-Away, a swing ride; Bert & Ernie's Watering hole, a water play area, and Air Grover, a children's roller coaster.

Stanleyville

This section of the park is home to the park's water rides and SheiKra, which was the first and only Dive Coaster in the United States until the addition of Griffon at the sister park Busch Gardens

Williamsburg. The section opened up in 1973 with the addition of the Stanley Falls Flume. The African Queen Boat Ride opened in 1977 as Busch's version of Disney's Jungle Cruise. In 1989, the African Queen Boat Ride was transformed into Tanganyika Tidal Wave with the addition of a 55-foot drop that generates a giant splash. The section remained unchanged from then until 2005, when SheiKra opened, and the surrounding area was renovated.

Sheikra

A 200-foot Bolliger & Mabillard floorless dive roller coaster with a 90-degree vertical drop. This is Florida's first Floorless Vertical Dive Coaster.

Stanley Falls Flume, a log flume with a 43-foot drop.

Tanganyika Tidal Wave, a 20 passenger shoot the

chutes water ride with a 55-foot drop.

Congo
Python, the park's first roller coaster. It was also Florida's first inverting roller coaster. It was removed in 2006.

This section contains two of the park's more popular rides. In November 2006, Congo underwent major renovation, including the removal of the park's classic Python roller coaster.

Kumba, meaning roar in Swahili, is a 143-foot steel sit-down roller coaster with seven inversions. Built in 1993 by Bolliger & Mabillard, it still remains a popular ride today.

Congo River Rapids, a water ride that simulates raging whitewater rapids. The ride opened in 1982.

Ubanga Banga Bumper Cars, a bumper cars ride.

Jungala
Jungala is a 4-acre family attraction featuring up-close animal encounters, rope bridges to explore three stories of jungle life, and a water-play area for children. Also located in this area are two family attractions: Jungle Flyers, a zip line that offers three different flight patterns above the treetops of the new area, and Wild Surge, a shot tower that launches guests above a waterfall. Another attraction is Tiger Trail, which is a walkthrough with tigers where there is also a glass turret where you can look out right in the middle of the tiger enclosure. Stiltwalkers perform and interact with guests in the heart of Jungala during several parts of the day.

Jungle Fliers, a zip line ride.

The Wild Surge, a Moser family launch tower ride.

Python, an Arrow Dynamics looping coaster patterned after the original Corkscrew at Knott's Berry Farm, previously occupied the site occupied now by Jungala.

Timbuktu

A section themed after the malls and bazaars of Africa. The Phoenix was built in 1984 and remains a popular ride to this day. The section was renovated in

2003. Important rides added during this facelift included the Timbuktu Theater, which replaced the park's Dolphin Theater with an indoor 4-D movie theater. In 2004, Das Festhaus was transformed into the Desert Grill, and the park's family-friendly Sand Serpent wild mouse roller coaster opened, replacing the Crazy Camel flat ride.

Scorpion, a steel Schwarzkopf-designed sit-down roller coaster with one vertical loop.

Sand Serpent, a steel wild mouse roller coaster.

Phoenix, an Intamin Looping Starship themed as an Egyptian cargo vessel.

Sesame Street Film Festival 4-D a 3-D short film starring characters from Sesame Street. The film is shown in the Timbuktu Theater jointly with Pirates 4-D.

Pirates 4-D a 3-D short film about Pirates starring Leslie Nielsen. It is shown in the Timbuktu Theater jointly with Sesame Street.

Sandstorm, an orbiter ride with six arms that spins riders around. Sandstorm will be relocated to the plaza in front of the Gwazi twin coasters.

Caravan Carousel, a carousel with horses, camels, and chariots.

Nairobi

Alligators and crocodiles can be observed here up close. In Curiosity Cavern, guests can view mammal and reptile exhibits. Visitors to Nairobi can view injured or abandoned newborns at the Nairobi Field Station Animal Nursery. The area also contains Myombe Reserve, a tropical rainforest that is home to Western Lowland Gorillas and Common

Chimpanzees. The major ride here is Rhino Rally, an unpredictable off-road safari that once sent its riders down a raging river. The river portion of the attraction was eventually abandoned due to repeated vehicle breakdowns. In 2012 the Animal Care Center opened. The main train station at Busch Gardens is located at Nairobi. Another popular attraction here is the Asian Elephant exhibit, which is also featured in the Rhino Rally ride.

Rhino Rally, a Vekoma River Adventure ride, Riders board inside modified Land Rovers through the park's Serengeti Plain habitat, interacting with animals.

Animal Care Center, this nearly 16,000 square-foot attraction allows visitors the chance to view the Busch Gardens' veterinarians at work in a new state of the art veterinary hospital. The major visitor aspects of the facility include a nutrition demonstration kitchen, treatment rooms, a clinical lab and an interactive diagnostic activity. Behind the scenes the veterinary hospital also includes the animal nutrition center, animal recovery and holding rooms and vet offices. The park's former animal care center was located behind the scenes.

Crown Colony Plaza
Crown Colony House
Crown Colony is the smallest section of the park. It features a restaurant, the Cheetah Hunt roller coaster, and the Skyride station. 2009 marked the 50th anniversary of Busch Gardens, so a museum was set up, featuring a timeline of pictures, costumes from previous shows, and old maps of the park. It also has

a preserved Python roller coaster seat. The museum is still there today.

Cheetah Hunt A multi-launch steel roller coaster that opened in 2011.

Cheetah Run an animal exhibit located next to Cheetah Hunt. It replaced the Clydesdale Hamlet.

Egypt
Bedouin tents and authentic handicrafts and art create an Egyptian marketplace feel. Guests can visit a replica of King Tutankhamen's tomb with the excavation in progress. The primary attraction of the Egypt themed area is Montu, an inverted steel coaster.

Montu, named after the Egyptian Falcon God of War, is a 150-foot steel inverted Bolliger & Mabillard roller coaster with seven inversions.

ANIMAL EXHIBITS

Cheetah Run
In May 2011, Cheetah Run opened. Cheetah Run

is home to Busch Gardens Tampa Bay collection of Cheetahs. There are running demonstrations and meet a keeper throughout the day. In addition the exhibit has interactive screens with cheetah facts.

The Serengeti Plain

In 1965, the park opened its Serengeti Plain animal habitat, the first of its kind to offer animals in a free-roaming environment. Over the years, the habitat has expanded from 29-acre to its current size of 65-acre. It is home to the Grevy's zebra, reticulated giraffe, bongo, addax, White Rhinoceros, eland, impala, ostrich, marabou stork, East African crowned crane and sacred ibis.

Myombe Reserve
Giraffes at the "Edge of Africa" attraction.

A 3-acre home for six lowland gorillas and nine chimpanzees located in Nairobi, opened in 1992.

Edge of Africa

Opened in 1997, Edge of Africa is a walk-through attraction where guests can observe African animals. Among the exhibits are a Nile Crocodile, meerkats, two prides of lions, a pack of Spotted Hyenas, two hippos, vultures and a troop of lemurs.

Curiosity Caverns

This cavern attraction, formerly known as Nocturnal Mountain, contains animals such as bats, snakes, lizards, tamarins, and sugar gliders in the low-light environment. This attraction offers the true facts about the creatures inside and cracks the myths about them wide open.

Real Music Series
From January - March, Busch Gardens hosts a weekly concert series, which invites popular bands either in Big Bands or Pop to perform classic or contemporary songs.

Bands, Brew & BBQ

(Previously called Bud & BBQ) For the month of February, Busch Gardens hosts a series of concerts in Gwazi Field, from many classic and contemporary Country music acts; there are special culinary offerings along the walkway from the Gwazi Roller Coaster to the gate in Gwazi Field.

Viva La Musica!

In March, several Latin music acts, such as Guyacon, are hosted on the Stage in Gwazi Field. There is a similar culinary setup with special offerings for the concert days as there is for Bands, Brew & BBQ.

BOYD HILL NATURE PARK/PRESERVE

1101 Country Club Way S, St. Petersburg: 727-893-7326
www.stpeteparksrec.org/boyd-hill-nature-preserve.html
ADMISSION: fees vary
HOURS: Tues - Fri & Sun 9 a.m. - 7 p.m., Sat 7 a.m. – 7 p.m., Closed Monday.
Preserve closes at 6 p.m. November through February
Boyd Hill Nature Park & Preserve, more than three miles of trails and boardwalks, contains 5 unique ecosystems: hardwood hammocks, sand pine scrub, pine flatwoods, willow marsh and lake shore. The park is part of the Great Florida Birding Trail. This park is a favorite of birdwatchers and butterfly lovers. A park highlight is the Ripple Effect, an interactive exhibit showcasing Boyd Hill's distinct ecosystems and how every action has an equal or greater reaction in our environment. Onsite bird of prey aviary. The park includes picnic areas, a playground and a gift shop. Guided tours are available as well as group rentals and overnight camping facilities.

CALADESI ISLAND
1 Causeway Blvd, Dunedin, 727-469-5918
www.floridastateparks.org/park/Caladesi-Island
ADMISSION: Varies
Catch the ferry at Honeymoon Island State Park for entrance onto Caladesi Island. Entrance fees at Honeymoon Island State Park apply.
The ferry travels to Caladesi Island for a four-hour stay. Fees vary.

Caladesi is one of the few completely natural islands along Florida's Gulf Coast. Beach lovers can enjoy swimming, sunbathing and beachcombing. Saltwater anglers can cast a line from their boats or surf fish. Nature enthusiasts can spot wildlife while hiking the three-mile nature trail through the island's interior or paddling a three mile kayak trail through the mangroves and bay. Picnic tables and shelters are located near the beach, and picnic pavilions can be reserved for a fee. The park has a marina with electric and water hookups, as well as a snack bar and gift shop. The park is accessible by boat or ferry.

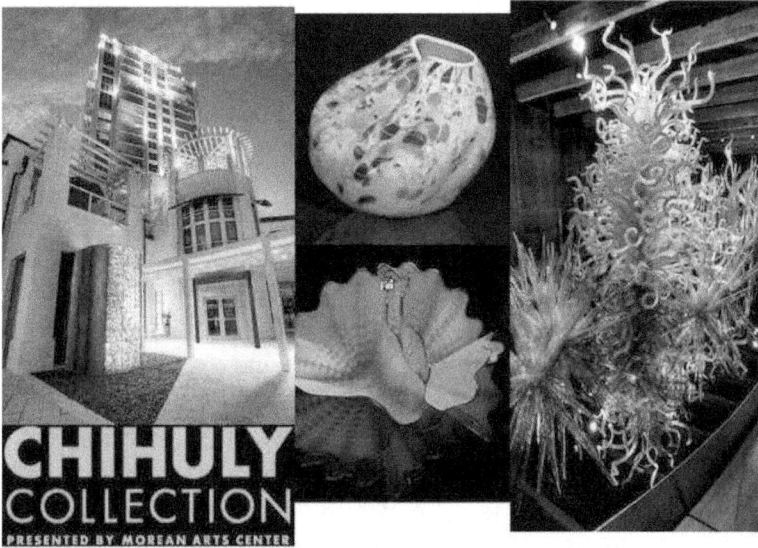

CHIHULY COLLECTION

720 Central Ave, St. Petersburg, 727-822-7872
www.visitstpeteclearwater.com/art-galleries/chihuly-collection/427
ADMISSION & Hours vary.
The CHIHULY COLLECTION is a stunning, permanent collection of world-renowned artist Dale Chihuly's unique artwork in a magnificent 10,000 square foot setting designed by award-winning architect Albert Alfonso. Guests are welcomed at the entrance by the iconic 20-foot sculpture created specifically for the site. The Collection includes Chihuly's spectacular large-scale installations such as Ruby Red Icicle Chandelier along with series works including Macchia, Ikebana, Niijima Floats, Persians and Tumbleweeds. 30-seat theater shows an informative video presentation. Admission to the

Chihuly Store is free without visiting the Chihuly Collection.

CLEARWATER MARINE AQUARIUM
249 Windward Psge, Clearwater, 727-441-1790
www.seewinter.com
ADMISSION fees vary
HOURS: Monday – Sunday: 9 a.m. – 6 p.m.
The Clearwater Marine Aquarium (in what used to be a wastewater treatment facility) is dedicated to the rescue and rehabilitation of marine mammals and sea turtles.

Exhibits include otters, sea turtles, sharks, stingrays, mangroves, and sea grass. This facility also features a series of education programs, from dolphin encounters to trainer-for-a-day programs.

One popular attraction is the **Sea Life Safari**, a 2-hour boat trip that scouts dolphins, sea birds, and other marine life en route to a shell island.

Maybe you've heard of **Winter**, the bottlenose dolphin that lost its tail and was retrofitted with a replacement fashioned from silicone and plastic. The story was told in the 2011 film "**Dolphin Tale**," shot here on location. A local business college study shows the movie will have brought in some $1.7 billion in revenue as tourists flock to see Winter, with attendance up by 4 times the usual rate to 750,000 last year.

A photo with Winter or pals Hope or Panama, costs a fee. Or buy the "trainer for a day" package. Unforgettable experience.

CURTIS HIXON WATERFRONT PARK

600 N Ashley Dr, Tampa, 813-274-8615
www.visittampabay.com/listings/curtis-hixon-waterfront-park/7676/
NEIGHBORHOOD: Downtown Tampa
Popular park for locals and tourists with great water features, a small dog park, and the river walk passes through the park. Great place for a family outing or picnic.

DALI MUSEUM
One Dali Blvd., St. Petersburg, 727-823-3767
www.thedali.org
ADMISSION: fees vary
The Dali Museum Collection features works from artist Salvador Dali's entire career (1904-1989). The Collection includes 96 oil paintings, many original drawings, bookworks, prints, sculpture, photos, manuscripts, and an extensive archive of documents. Founded with the works collected by Reynolds and Eleanor Morse, the Museum has made significant additions to its collection.

EDISON & FORD WINTER ESTATES
2350 McGregor Blvd., Fort Myers, 239-334-7419
www.edisonfordwinterestates.org/
TOURS: open from 9 to 5:30, with the last guided tour setting off at 4.

I know it's nowhere near Clearwater or St., Pete, but I was so taken with this place that if I were in Clearwater, I'd rent a car and drive down for half a day.

It's just as well these two estates share a common name now their owners are dead, because Thomas Edison and Henry Ford were such great friends in life. It all started in 1885, when Edison came to what was no more than a tiny settlement on the Caloosahatchee River. Here he bought 14 acres and started building his house and factory where he continued his work inventing things. (His principal residence was in West Orange, N.J.).

Friends like Henry Ford and Harvey Firestone visited him and bought parcels nearby so they could enjoy the beautiful Florida winter climate Edison had embraced. Ford bought his house in 1916, and you'll get to see the splendid view of the Caloosahatchee River that Ford enjoyed from the "Ford Porch."

The complex joins the Ford house next door, and now includes about 20 acres of historical buildings, very special gardens (Edison collected plant specimens and people sent them to him from all over the world—he planted them here in botanical gardens that remain to this day).

Here you'll see the Edison Main House, the Guest House he built for long-term visitors, the Edison Botanic Research Lab and the Edison Ford Museum, which offers an impressive array of inventions, artifacts and special exhibit galleries.

Fascinating is the banyan tree you encounter right after the parking lot. It looks on first glance to be a hammock or a small forest of trees, but really all the trunks are aerial roots of the same tree, a tree Edison himself planted in 1925. A sign tells you that it was sent to Edison by Firestone, who knew that one of Edison's goals was to generate a source for rubber here in the U.S. so America wouldn't have to rely on foreign sources in the event of a war that could cut off our supply. (Remember, Firestone made tires!)

You'll be interested to see that when Thomas Edison took a "vacation," it most certainly was a working vacation. His lab had room not only for himself, but a group of scientists he brought down to work with him. He never stopped.

There's an exhibit detailing Edison's camping trips into the Everglades with Ford. Ford even supplied a motorized "chuck wagon," adapting one of his cars into perhaps the first RV which was loaded with food and supplies to accompany them on their adventures into the wild.

FLORIDA AQUARIUM
701 Channelside Dr., Tampa: 813-273-4000
www.flaquarium.org/
COST: fees vary, depending on the package you want. Check web site to see if they're any discounts. Here you'll encounter some 20,000 marine creatures in an amazing setting. They show you how (as you follow it on its path) a drop of water goes from the wetlands through the mangroves and on into the bay. You end up looking through a 40-foot wide window into the Coral Reefs exhibit where there are hundreds of varieties of fish life.
The Wild Dolphin Cruise. Tampa Bay is home to more than 500 bottlenose dolphins and is one of the best places in Florida to view endangered manatees

and numerous species of birds, many of which are threatened or endangered. All of this wildlife thrives in one of the busiest deepwater ports in the Southern United States. The 90-minute **Eco-tour** through the bay aboard their 72-foot catamaran, the *Bay Spirit II,* allows you to encounter the awesome animals that thrive in these local waters. A good pair of binoculars is a good idea.

Penguins: Backstage Pass is a fun and educational 30-minute experience where you get the chance to interact with penguins in an up-close and personal setting.

Dive with the Sharks provides a unique opportunity for certified SCUBA divers, age 15 and older, to come face-to-face with live sharks. Dive into the Aquarium's largest tank, the Coral Reef Exhibit; warm clear water, teeming with massive sharks, moray eels, barracudas, a green sea turtle, etc. They provide all of your gear.

Swim with the Fishes, an in-water reef experience, gives visitors 6 and older an adventure on a replica of one of the Florida Keys' most beautiful coral reef dive sites without being a certified SCUBA diver.

FLORIDA FREE RIDES
727-424-5458
www.floridafreerides.com
HOURS: Open 7 days a week from 9 a.m. – 3 a.m.
FloridaFreeRides.com is an environmentally friendly transportation service that gives rides for free anywhere on Clearwater Beach, including Sand Key & Island Estates. The vehicles are paid for by sponsorships & the team works for tips.

FLORIDA HOLOCAUST MUSEUM

55 5th St. S, St. Petersburg: 727-820-0100

www.flholocaustmuseum.org

ADMISSION: fees vary

Free docent-led tours are available every Wednesday and Sunday at 2 pm.

The Florida Holocaust Museum features both permanent and temporary exhibitions. The first floor houses the History, Heritage and Hope Permanent Exhibition. The second-floor galleries house the Museum's temporary exhibition program with rotating exhibitions. The Museum focuses on contemporary artwork about the Holocaust, other genocides and human rights issues. Kane's Furniture Hall, on the third floor, features temporary and permanent exhibitions like Kaddish in Wood, woodcarvings of French children of the Holocaust created by Dr. Herbert Savel. Temporary exhibitions in Kane's Furniture Hall include small history exhibitions as well as student-created artwork.

FLORIDA ORANGE GROVES AND WINERY

1500 Pasadena Ave. S, S Pasadena, 727-347-4025

www.floridawine.com

ADMISSION: Free

Wine tastings are available daily from 9:30 a.m. until 5 p.m. Tours are given upon request if guides are available.

Florida Orange Groves and Winery is a licensed wine manufacturer, distributor, and retailer of unique, culturally significant Florida wine and premium wine products currently producing 37 varieties of wine.

Sample delicious wines made from mangoes or red raspberries.

GREEN BENCH BREWING CO.

1133 Baum Ave N, St Petersburg, 727-800-9836
www.greenbenchbrewing.com
NEIGHBORHOOD: Downtown St Petersburg
A popular craft brewery featuring an impressive selection of ales and stouts. You have order a flight so you can try several of the 10 or so brews at one sitting. Large beer garden and side deck with a great collection of games.

GULF BEACHES HISTORICAL MUSEUM

115 10th Ave, St. Pete Beach, 727-552-1610
http://gulfbeachesmuseum.com
ADMISSION: Free
HOURS: 10 – 4, Fri - Sun
Located in what once was the first church in the tiny village of Pass-a-Grill, built in 1917, this museum celebrates the early life of the South Pinellas beach communities. It's at the very end of the barrier island. Joan Haley, an early conservationist, saved the church and gave it to the county as a museum. Old post cards, vintage photos from the early 1900s, exhibits from WW 2, and there's a nicely stocked store here where you can buy books about local history, jewelry and stock up on free brochures.

HENRY B. PLANT MUSEUM

401 W. Kennedy Blvd. (bet. Hyde Park & Magnolia),
Tampa: 813-254-1891
www.plantmuseum.com

Florida has always been home to a bunch of eccentric
millionaires. One of them built this place. Henry Plant
was a railroad baron from the Gilded Age. He was to
Florida's West Coast what Henry Flagler was to the
East Coast.

In 1891, Plant built this faux Moorish palace
(inspired quite obviously by the Alhambra) as the
500-room Tampa Bay Hotel to draw tourists here.
(He succeeded.) There are 13 minarets rising above
this unusual building.

A spur of Plant's rail line extended to the hotel.
Riders could leave the train and walk right into the
lobby.

While you might just glance sat the building as a
curiosity when you drive by, it's well worth your time
to go inside where you'll find some of the rooms of

the old hotel painstakingly restored so you get to see what they really looked like when the place was new.

JOLLEY TROLLEY
410 N. Myrtle Ave., Clearwater, 727-445-1200
www.clearwaterjolleytrolley.com
ADMISSION: fees vary
HOURS: Friday, Saturday & Sunday.
The perfect alternative for your transportation needs from Clearwater Beach to Tarpon Springs. Runs between Clearwater Beach and Downtown Clearwater, Dunedin, Palm Harbor and Tarpon Springs.

THE LOBBY BAR
@The Don CeSar
3400 Gulf Blvd, In The Don CeSar, St. Pete Beach, 727-360-1881
www.doncesar.com/
NEIGHBORHOOD: St Pete Beach
Great spot for an after-dinner cocktail. Usually live jazz.

MAHAFFEY THEATER

400 1st St. S, St. Petersburg: 727-892-5767
www.themahaffey.com
ADMISSION: Check website for ticket prices.
Located in downtown St. Petersburg, the Mahaffey
Theater is a 2,031 seat cultural center featuring
elegant ballroom space, spectacular waterfront views,
and European box-style seating. The Mahaffey hosts
top-quality national and international artists and
performances including Broadway, classical, pop,
rock, comedy, dance, family, and the renowned
Florida Orchestra. The theater first opened in 1965.

MOSI

4801 E. Fowler Ave, Tampa: 813-987-6000
www.mosi.org
You may need more than a Long Weekend just to
explore this place with its 400+ interactive exhibits.

KIDS IN CHARGE. For kids 12 and under, this is the place. Based on cutting-edge theories about learning and skill building, Kids In Charge emphasizes the value of learning through play by bringing together science, creative thinking and inspire the imagination. With a total size of 40,000 square feet, including 25,000 square feet of exhibit space, Kids In Charge is the largest children's science center in the country.

DISASTERVILLE. MOSI's permanent exhibit, "Disasterville" is a 10,000-square-foot dramatic and engaging public exhibition where you're able to walk through interactive towns and experience the impact of a variety of simulated natural disasters. Disasterville covers nine types of disasters: floods, hail storms, hurricanes, lightning, tornadoes, wildfires, volcanoes, earthquakes and tsunamis. Learn how to take action and minimize the effects of nature's fury in your life.
Experience thrilling simulated presentations that detail the use of appropriate materials and necessary precautions taken during an impending natural disaster.

WEATHERQUEST. Here you get to step into the role of a weather reporter, engineer or even producer in Bay News 9 Weather*Quest*—an interactive news-assignment exhibit allowing visitors the chance to oversee an entire weather broadcast from a real-life news desk and meteorologist green screen. Located with the *Disasterville* exhibition area, Weather*Quest* is a "team-oriented" mission-based program meant to introduce you to the extreme detail and research put into weather reporting and geological forecasting. You can step into the roles of weather reporter, anchor, emergency manager, producer, or scientist within a newsroom designed as mock Bay News 9 studio. In addition, Weather*Quest* features a glass front so other MOSI guests can observe the newsroom in action. These are just some of the things going on here. Don't pass it by.

MUSEUM OF FINE ARTS
255 Beach Dr. NE, St. Petersburg: 727-896-2667
www.fine-arts.org
ADMISSION: fees vary
The Museum of Fine Arts, one of the most beautiful museums in the Southeast, houses a collection of more than 14,000 objects extending from antiquity to the present day and features stellar French Impressionist paintings. Galleries feature Steuben glass, decorative arts, and pre-Columbian objects. The museum has two interior gardens, one devoted to sculpture and the other displays works on paper and photographs. The museum features a legendary permanent collection as well as traveling exhibitions. This is the only comprehensive art collection of its kind on Florida's west coast with work from Monet, Cézanne, and Renoir. Onsite museum store and MFA Café.

THE PALLADIUM AT ST PETERSBURG COLLEGE
253 5th Ave. N, St. Petersburg: 727-822-3590

www.mypalladium.org/
ADMISSION: Check website for event schedule and ticket prices.
The historic Palladium Theater, located in downtown St. Petersburg's cultural center, is ranked as one of Tampa Bay's best and most affordable venues for a wide range of entertainment including classical, jazz, blues, theatre, opera, Celtic, comedy, and dance.

PASS-A-GRILLE BEACH
St Pete Beach, 727-403-6136
www.visitpassagrille.com
Located near Lowe's Don Cesar Hotel, this beach features beautiful white sand, a local on-site grill, lots of restaurants, shopping, tennis courts, and fishing piers.

SAND KEY PARK
1060 Gulf Blvd., Clearwater, 727-582-2100
www.pinellascounty.org/park/15_sand_key.htm
ADMISSION: Automated pay stations are installed, with daily parking fees. A fee is not collected from persons entering the park on foot or by bicycle.
HOURS: 7 a.m. to sunset.
A beautiful park with a beach and a park equipped with grills, picnic tables, and water fountains. Park has a salt marsh with view benches, here you may see wildlife like heron, roseate spoonbill, great horned owl, anhinga, and common moorhen.

SAWGRASS LAKE PARK
7400 25th St. N, St. Petersburg: 727-217-7256
www.pinellascounty.org/park/16_Sawgrass.htm

ADMISSION: Free

The 400-acre Sawgrass Lake Park is one of the largest maple swamps on the Gulf Coast of Florida. This park, via the mile-long boardwalk and half-mile dirt trail, allows people the opportunity to walk through the swamp and see birds, butterflies, plants and animals in their natural settings within the most densely populated county in Florida. Birders and eco-tourists travel to this park to see the thousands of birds that migrate through the park during fall and spring. A variety of wildlife like herons, egrets, ibis, wood storks, alligators and turtles can be spotted along the canals and lakes.

SIM CENTER
483 Mandalay Ave. #200
2nd Floor in Pelican Plaza, Clearwater, 727-643-1781
www.simcentertampabay.com
ADMISSION: Rates and schedules vary.

HOURS: Call to schedule.

Here you can practice a takeoff and landing in the cockpit of a Boeing 737 simulator. The Dunedin flight center currently houses three flight simulators: a Boeing 737 jetliner, an F-16 and an F-35 fighter jet simulator, which you can fly in pre-scheduled time slots. The two fighter jets are linked together so that a team of 2 can complete a mission together.

ST. PETERSBURG MUSEUM OF HISTORY

335 2nd Ave. NE, St. Petersburg: 727-894-1052

www.spmoh.com

ADMISSION: fees vary

Since 1920, the St. Petersburg Historical Society, the oldest cultural organization in St. Petersburg, has operated this museum celebrating the culture and heritage of the Tampa Bay area. The museum house four galleries, two hold permanent exhibitions while the other two feature rotating exhibitions that change every four to six months. The museum has over 30,000 artifacts and archives in collections that help tell the history of the city. The museum is located on the waterfront at Vinoy Basin.

SUNKEN GARDENS

1825 4th St. N, St. Petersburg: 727-551-3102
www.stpete.org/sunken
ADMISSION: fees vary
Free parking on site. All areas handicap accessible.
For tour information call 727-551-3102
Sunken Gardens, St. Peterburg's oldest living
museum, is a botanical paradise set in the midst of a
bustling city. Here in this 100-year-old garden you'll
find some of the oldest tropical plants in the region as
well as exotic plants from around the world. Strolling
the meandering paths, you see cascading waterfalls,
beautiful demonstration gardens and an assortment of
over 50,000 tropical plants and flowers.

SUNSETS AT PIER 60
10 Pier 60, Clearwater Beach, 727-434-6060
www.sunsetsatpier60.com
ADMISSION: Free
HOURS: Hours 4:30 - 8:30 p.m., 7 Days a week
The Sunsets at Pier 60 Festival is a nightly sunset
celebration and impromptu (well, they're not really
that "impromptu") street performances with artisans,
crafts people and musical entertainment, weather
permitting. You get a Key West style sunset without
the long drive down. If you don't fancy the colorful
weirdos you will see here, you can opt for something
a little on the quieter side. Go to **Sand Key Park**, for
example. It's just a little south of Clearwater Beach.
Another choice might be **Caladesi Island** farther up
north. Here you'll find 3 miles of pristine beach but
you need to get there by private boat. Or the Caladesi
Island Ferry. www.caladesiferry.com

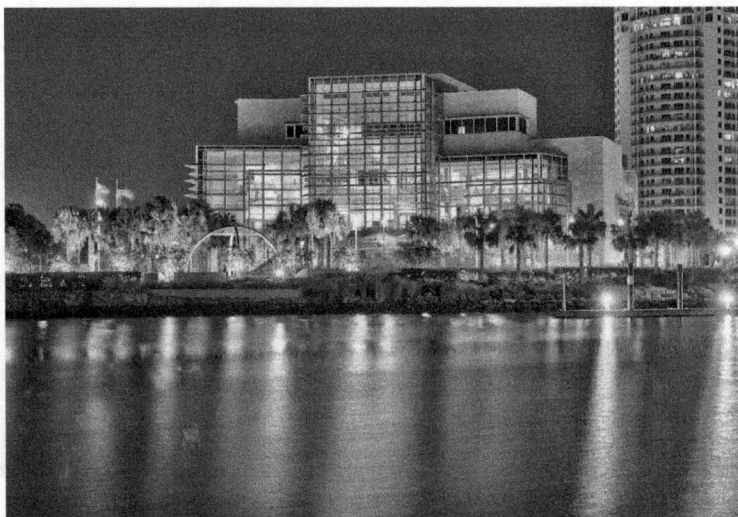

TAMPA BAY HISTORY CENTER
801 Old Water St, Tampa: 813-228-0097
www.tampabayhistorycenter.org
Inside the 60,000-square-foot History Center in
Tampa's bustling Channelside District you can take a
journey through 12,000 years of powerful stories.
Follow in the footsteps of the first native inhabitants,
Spanish conquistadors, pioneers, sports legends and
railroad tycoons. During your journey, you will stroll
through a 1920s-era cigar store, row up the
Hillsborough River, ride along with a cattle drive and
learn about the early exploration of Florida in a
dramatic theater presentation. Explore exhibits about
the places and people who shaped the Tampa Bay
area. The waterfront History Center boasts a stunning
atrium, interactive and immersive exhibits, theaters,
map gallery, research center, event hall, an eclectic
Museum Store and a restaurant, the **Columbia Cafe**.

The history of the Tampa Bay region comes alive within these walls, where your initial impressions of Tampa will change forever. (It certainly opened my eyes.)

TARPON SPRINGS HISTORICAL MUSEUM
160 E. Tarpon Ave., Tarpon Springs, 727-943-4624
www.tarponspringsareahistoricalsociety.org
ADMISSION: Free
HOURS: Wednesday - Saturday from 11a.m. to 4 p.m.
This museum celebrates the railroad with exhibits on education, health care, local institutions, and many more. The museum and gift shop is the railroad depot restored by the Tarpon Springs Area Historical Society.

WEEDON ISLAND PRESERVE
1800 Weedon Dr. NE, St. Petersburg: 727-453-6500
www.weedonislandpreserve.org
ADMISSION: Free
Hours: Thurs – Sat, 9 a.m. – 4 p.m.
A 3,190-acre natural preserve located on Tampa Bay comprised mostly of marine ecosystems with some uplands. The preserve protects a wide diversity of natural and cultural resources and is also a well-known birding and fishing site.

INDEX

www.ingramcontent.com/pod-product-compliance
Lightning Source LLC
La Vergne TN
LVHW021411080426
835508LV00020B/2560